THE PEOPLE'S PURGE

Also by Jessie Reyez

Words of a Goat Princess

WORDS OF A GOAT PRINCESS VOL. II

THE PEOPLE'S PURGE

Jessie Reyez

Andrews McMeel
PUBLISHING®

To anyone who calls out into the void
hoping for an answer.

Contents

INTRODUCTION ix

Love
1

Life
59

Mental Health
115

Creativity
155

ACKNOWLEDGMENTS 187
ABOUT THE AUTHOR 189
ABOUT THE ILLUSTRATOR 191
INDEX 193

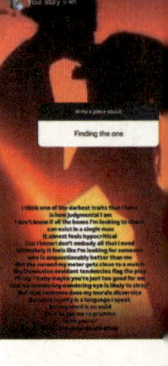

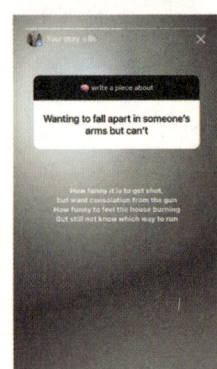

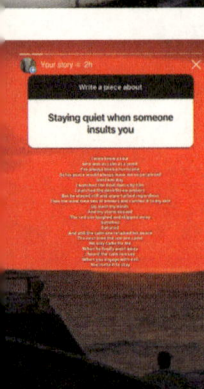

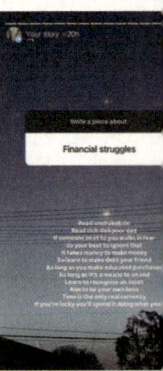
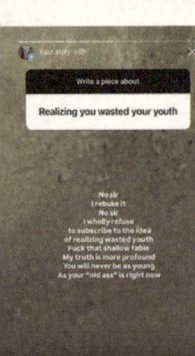
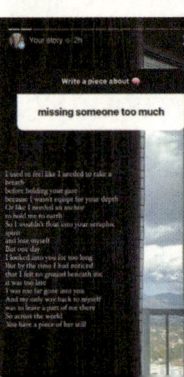
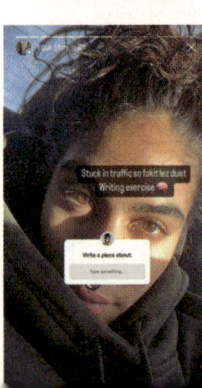

INTRODUCTION

The natural state of rhythm for the artist is to "create and release." However, when following due process for writing songs or books, time and patience and plans become a requisite; so my artistic rhythm was shackled. It felt impossible to get that (borderline narcissistic) itch scratched as desperately and as quickly as my inner child—the original artist—needed. Then it dawned on me. The cure for my poetic impediment landed in my hands . . . literally. An Instagram prompt "write a piece about" posed to an ocean of strangers with whom I somehow share a nebulous yet familiar intimacy. You gave me answers that would act as my arrow to point the way to artistic relief and delivered me the genesis of these pages. Of course, the artist and perfectionist in me has chiseled away a bit more at the marble, but the rawness remains.

Prompts from you, poems from me.

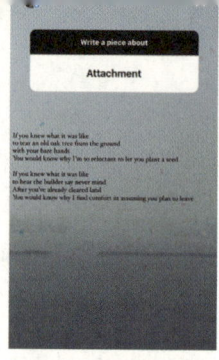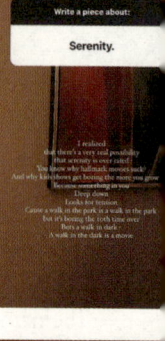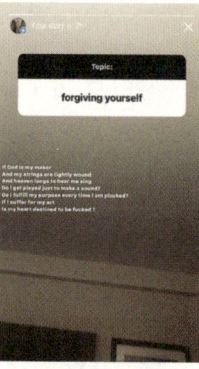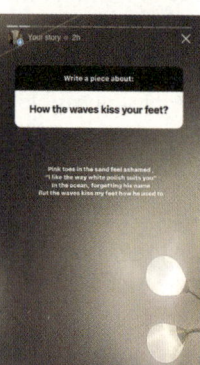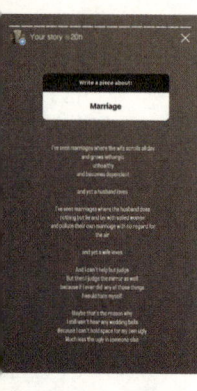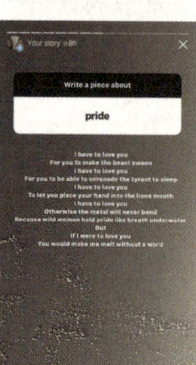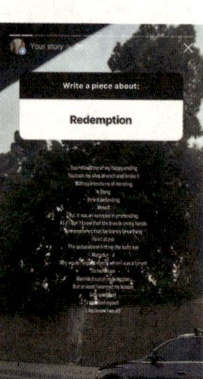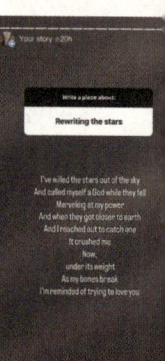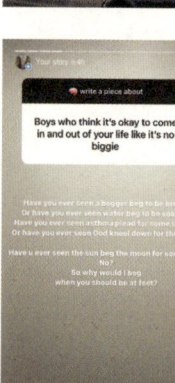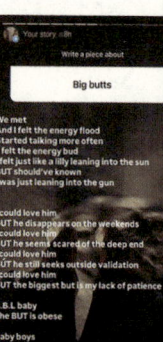

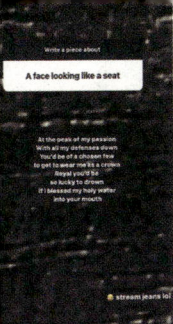
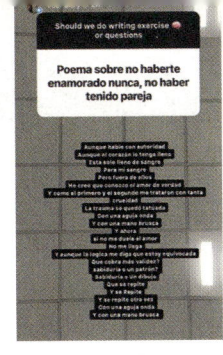
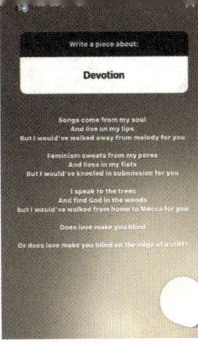

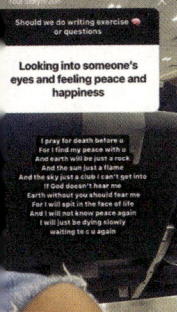

Love

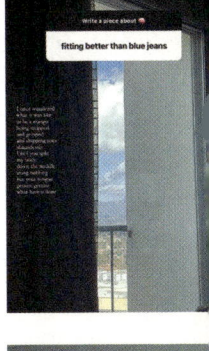
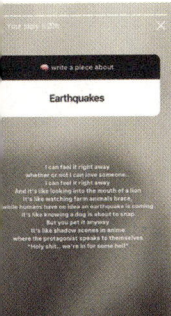
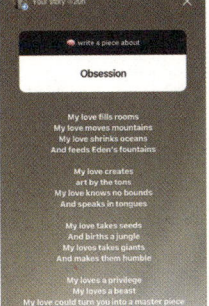

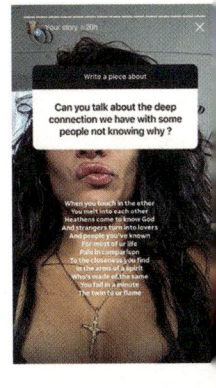

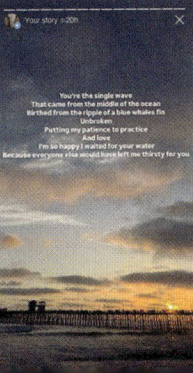
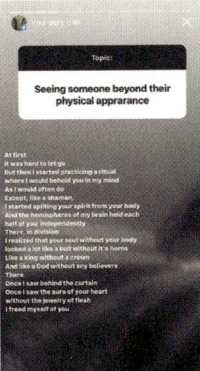

Write a piece about

Devotion

Songs come from my soul
And live on my lips
But I would've murdered melodies for you
Feminism sweats from my pores
And lives in my fists
But I would've kneeled in submission for you
I find God in the woods
And I speak to the trees
But I would've walked barefoot to Mecca for you
"Love makes you blind"
Nah
That ain't it
More like love makes you blind on the edge of a cliff

Write a piece about

Using your weakness against you

I showed you my belly
Knowing you had your fangs
Because I thought that your heart
Had more blood than your hands
But you can't blame a beast
For looking for food
And I can't blame my soft soul
For falling for you

Write a piece about

Rewriting the stars

I've willed the stars out of the sky
And called myself a god while they fell
Marveling at my power
But when they got closer to earth
And I reached out to catch one
It crushed me
Now
Under its weight
As my bones break
I am reminded of trying to love you

> **Write a piece about**
>
> **A face looking like a seat**

At the peak of my passion
With all my defenses down
You'd be one of a chosen few
to get to wear me as a crown
Royal you would be
And so lucky to drown
if I blessed my holy water
Right into your unholy mouth

Write a piece about

Unrequired love

I know you meant "unrequited"
Which means unanswered love
Unreturned love
Unreciprocated love
But the irony in your typo
is so loud
That a mistake gave you your answer
As life usually does
And sometimes
Once you learn to hold your own heart correctly
Someone else's unworthy hand
will feel like a shoe that's too tight
And being alone
will suddenly feel
like a relief

> **Write a piece about**
>
> **How the waves kiss your feet?**

Pink toes in the sand feel ashamed,
"I like the way white polish suits you"
In the ocean, forgetting his name
But the waves kiss my feet how he used to

Write a piece about

Seeing someone beyond their physical appearance

At first
it was hard to let go
But then I started practicing a ritual
where I would behold
you in my mind
As I would often do
except
like a shaman
I started splitting your spirit from your body
And the hemispheres of my brain
held each half of you independently
There
in division
I realized that your soul without your body
looked a lot like a bull without its horns
Like a king without a crown
And like a god without any believers
There
Once I saw behind the curtain
Once I saw the aura of your heart
without the jewelry of your flesh
I freed myself of you

Write a piece about

Reconnecting w/ an old love

You said you needed to work things out with her
And my love withered
A veiled woman fit your mind's ideal
much more than my sinning soul
I bent backward to find enough self-control not to message you
But a clean break was too much for you to execute
You pop up
"Hi"
I stare at my phone
Praying that my heart could morph into stone
But I break
as quickly and as brittle as a sun-dried bone
I ask if you're still together
I brace
"Yes. I'm sorry."
My heart breaks
Again
I reply, "OK"
"They were playing your song at the gym today"
I gather my wit
"that's God showing you we belong together,
but you're being a bitch"
You laugh at my joke
"Your sense of humor is what I miss most"
And just before a convo can even begin
In a couple of sentences
you're gone again

Write a piece about

Right person wrong time

I have as much patience as a grape has wine
I don't have it right now but maybe I'll have it in time

Write a piece about

Marriage

I've seen marriages where the wife scrolls all day
grows lethargically unhealthy
and becomes dependent
and yet the husband still loves
I've seen marriages where the husband does
nothing but lie and lay with other women
and pollute their own marriage
with no regard for the air
and yet the wife still loves
I can't help but judge
But my mirror isn't spared
because if I ever did any of those things
I would come to hate myself
Maybe that's the reason why
I likely won't hear wedding bells
I can't hold space for my own ugly
Much less the ugly in someone else

Write a piece about

Attachment

If you knew what it was like
to tear a banyan tree from the ground
with your bare hands
You would know why I'm so reluctant to let you plant a seed
If you knew what it was like
to hear the builder say "never mind"
after you've already cleared land
You would know why I find comfort in assuming you plan to leave

Write a piece about

Becoming the best version of yourself

My love raises the dead
But I've been warned to leave it alone
"Stop trying to give food to the needy
When the truth is you're starving at home"

> **Write a piece about**
>
> **Poema sobre no haberte enamorado nunca, no haber tenido pareja**

Aunque hable con autoridad
Aunque el corazón lo tenga lleno
Está solo lleno de sangre
Para mi sangre
O sea
Para mi familia
Pero fuera de ellos
No creo que conozca el amor de verdad
Y como el primero y el segundo me trataron con tanta crueldad
El trauma se quedó tatuado
Con una aguja honda
Y con una mano brusca
Y ahora
si no me duele el amor
No me llega
Y aunque la lógica me diga que estoy equivocada
¿Que cobra más validez?
¿sabiduría o un patron
Sabiduría o un dibujo
Que se repite
Y se repite
Y se repite otra vez
Con una aguja honda
Y con una mano brusca

Write a piece about

How I can't fall in love with nobody

Although I speak with authority
over matters of the heart
And though my heart is full
I fear it is only full of blood
For my own blood
Because outside of them
I don't think I know true love
And since my first and my second
handled me with cruelty
The trauma got ingrained
The trauma got tatted
And the needle was long
And the hand of the artist was rough
And now
If love doesn't hurt me
It doesn't feel valid
And cannot penetrate beyond my chest
And though logic tells me I am wrong
What's more valid: logic or a pattern?
Logic or a pattern drawn over
And over
And over again
Tatted
With a long, long needle
and a heavy, heavy hand

Write a piece about

Feeling stuck but everyone thinks you are moving forward

In the north,
The snowbanks claim cars
like memories claim the brain of a broken heart
Engines rev
Wheels spin
But nothing moves
Stuck
Until time gives way despite herself
And warmth comes hidden in the hour
Finally
The ice gives charity
The wheels catch friction
And the car is off
Free
But then the speakers spill out our song

... stuck again

Write a piece about

Infatuation

To be inclined to infatuation
Is to kneel at the foot of a ruthless giant
Whose age is nowhere near their size
Whose brain is filled with neon colors
And mirrors
And no sense of time
Who eats what it pleases but never shares food with you
Yet begs you to stay for dinner
so they can watch you watch them eat
Because they love how you look when you're hungry

Write a piece about

Fitting better than blue jeans

I once wondered
what it was like
to be a mango
being stripped
and gripped
and dripping juice
shamelessly
Until you split
my body
down the middle
using nothing
but your tongue
gemini gemini
what have u done

Write a piece about

Boys who think it's OK to come in and out of your life like it's no biggie

Have you ever seen a beggar beg to be broke?
Or have you ever seen water beg to be soaked?
Have you ever seen asthma plead for some smoke?
Or have you ever seen God kneel down to the pope?
Have you ever seen the sun beg the moon for some heat?
So if I'm a whole feast
why would I beg for some meat?

Write a piece about

Loving someone that loves someone else

You'd think this would be the worst
But it's not
At least there's a human to tie your loss to
But losing someone to air?
Losing someone to the "potential" of another
is as low
as the knees of the ant that André 3000 wrote about
in one of my favorite Frank songs
"Solo"
Because it's not like they'd rather someone else over you
They'd rather no one
They'd rather space
At least your undertaker has a face

Write a piece about

Pride

I have to love you
For you to make the beast swoon
I have to love you
For you to be able to serenade the tyrant to sleep
I have to love you
To let you place your hand inside the lion's mouth
I have to love you
Otherwise the metal will never bend
Because wild women hold pride like breath underwater
But if I were to love you
I'd float at the sound of your voice

Write a piece about

Limerence

I'm scared to read the pages of your book
Because your cover says *lover* and I believe it a thousand times
I think I could lay with you a thousand nights and miss you still
Bold words to hold for a stranger whose skin I have yet to taste
So the words linger unspoken
On my tongue
Where you belong
The movies projected on the insides of my eyes all feature your face
The impact is coming
I guess I should brace
Maybe this time I'll love the runner
More than I've been known to love the chase

Write a piece about

Long-distance relationships

When you love from too close
Emotions get too sappy
When you love from far away
The four of you are happy

Write a piece about

Forgiving yourself

If God is my maker
And my strings are tightly wound
And heaven longs to hear me sing
Do I get played just to make a sound?
Do I fulfill my purpose every time I am plucked?
If I suffer for my art
Is my heart destined to be fucked?

Write a piece about

Redemption

You robbed me of my happy ending
You took my olive branch and broke it
With no intentions of mending
a thing
I tried defending
Myself
But it was an exercise in pretending
As if I don't know that the blood's on my hands
And memories that lay barely breathing
Point at me
The accusations hitting the bullseye
Matadora
"Why would you expect mercy when you were a tyrant?"
I stand in front of you silent
Gambled out of my redemption
But at least I learned my lesson
Amy said it best
I cheated myself
Like I knew I would

Write a piece about

Wanting to fall apart in someone's arms but can't

How funny it is to get shot
but want consolation from the gun
How funny to feel the house burning
but still not know which way to run

Write a piece about

Cutting ties w/ that one person

Out of sight
Out of mind
Is literally the best advice

Easy peasy
Who would've thought?
Just needed to hit you with a big ol' block

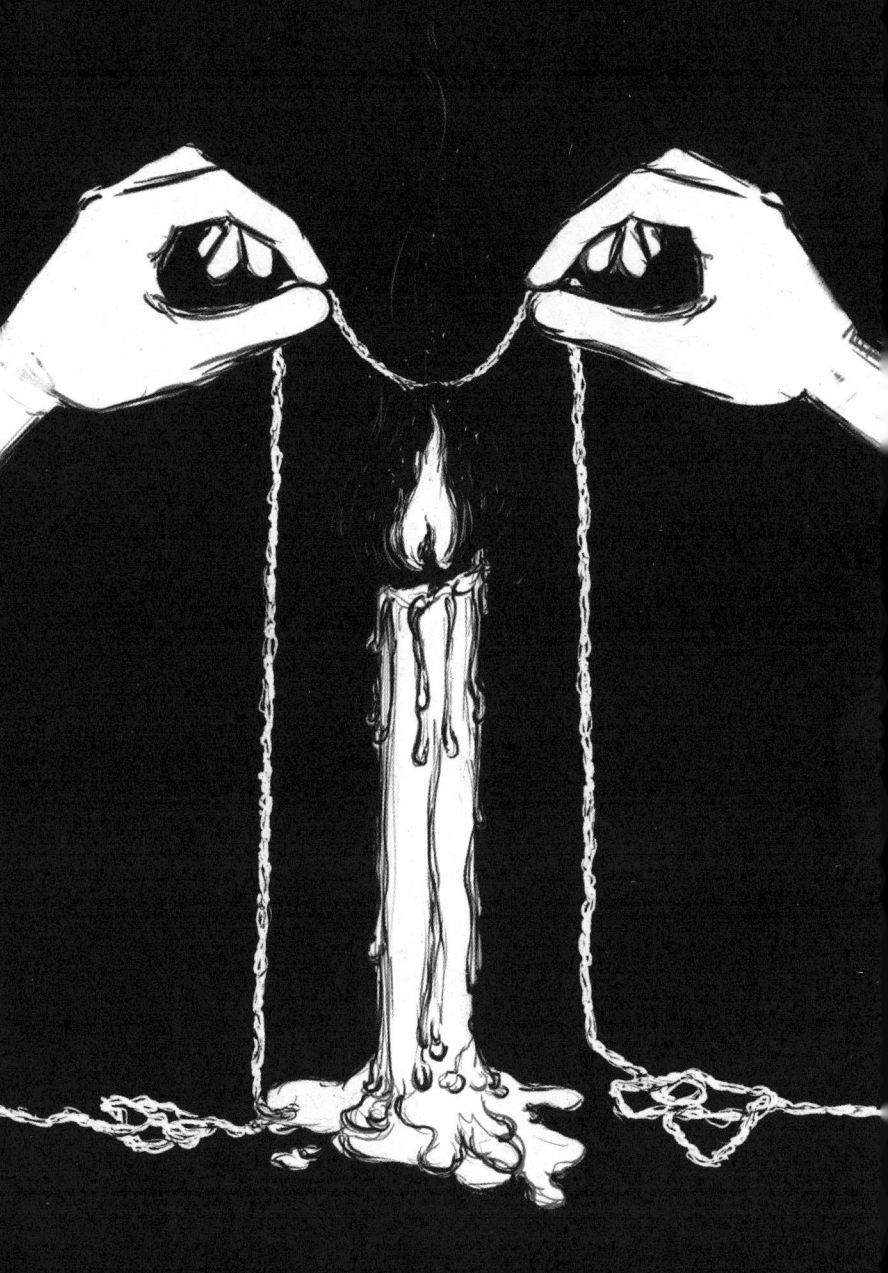

Write a piece about

Earthquakes

I can feel it right away
whether or not I can love someone
I can feel it right away
It's like looking into the mouth of a lion
or like watching farm animals brace
while humans have no idea an earthquake is on the way
It's like knowing a dog is about to snap
But petting it regardless

Write a piece about

Standing on the beach at sunset

You're the single wave
That came from the middle of the ocean
Birthed from the ripple of a blue whale's fin
Unbroken
Putting my patience to practice
And love
I'm so happy I waited for your water
Because everyone else would have left me thirsty

Write a piece about

Obsession

My love can fill rooms
My love can move mountains
My love can shrink oceans
and feed Eden's fountains
My love can create
But it can also destroy
So don't wake up my passion
if you still play with toys

Write a piece about

Breadcrumbs

Breadcrumbs work on the starving
But if you have food at home
Breadcrumbs will make you laugh
And say "nice try, bitch, leemelone"

Write a piece about
Mind-blowing things

Swimming butt naked in the ocean at night
Feeling the rush of love at first sight
Passion with someone that matches your freak
Tensing all muscles when you're at the peak
Jumping from a gondola up in the sky
Hearing a voice when you ask heaven why
Being out in the wild and petting a beast
Exposing your neck and letting Romeo feast

Write a piece about

Love

Deification through intimacy
has to be one of the sweetest sins I've ever tasted
I intend no irreverence to the God above me
But if being held in the clouds
for a measly morsel of time
by a single human
left me so euphoric
How honeyed it must be
to be held so high in the heavens by history
I see why God demands praise
I was once loved in this way
But it left me savoring a drop of blood
while I was just a carnivore in denial

Write a piece about

No contact

I gave your hoodie away
What's mine won't miss me
I saw a meme you would've liked yesterday
What's mine won't miss me
I was in your city but I didn't let you know
What's mine won't miss me
My best friend said I should just let it go
What's mine won't miss me

As much as I wish I could hold you
And as much as I wish you could kiss me
in this life
You're just not mine
So tell me, love,
do you miss me?

Write a piece about

Abandonment

"Goodbye" is just a word
But being left brokenhearted is the worst
So I found myself a safety net
nestled deep within a verb
"Leaving" before it hurts
Is the best solution that I've learned
That spares me from writing yet another
brokenhearted verse
It's a trope you might've heard
And it might not allot me what I deserve
But I'm happier these days
So at the very least
I know it works
Lol

Write a piece about

Your future husband

The thing most people forget about a strong woman
is that sometimes
sometimes
she will submit
willingly
eyes closed and in full faith
once she knows that she is in the hands
of a galvanizing man
But I refuse to raise another woman's son to become my partner

Match me or beat me
But beneath me
You'll never reach me

Write a piece about

Grief

Grief is only as deep
As the love was once profound
So when you stand over ruins
You also stand on once-fertile ground
Love leaves a hole
That's the price of touching the sun
Shot straight to the heart
That's the price of playing with guns

Write a piece about

Finding the one

One of the darkest traits I have
Is how judgmental I am
I don't know if the boxes I'm looking to check
Can all exist in a man
It almost feels hypocritical
Cuz I don't embody all that I need
Ultimately it feels like I'm looking for someone
Who is unquestionably better than me
But the second my meter gets close to a match
My dismissive avoidant shows face
"Baby maybe you're just too good for me
And my wandering eye's likely to stray"
But that does my morals no justice
Cuz loyalty is a language I speak
But my word is so solid
So to get me to promise
To be yours?
Babe
the chances are bleak

> **Write a piece about**
>
> **The deep connection we have with some people not knowing why**

When you touch in the ether
You melt into each other
Heathens come to know God
And strangers turn into lovers
And people you've known
For most of your life
Pale in comparison
To the closeness you find
in the arms of a spirit
Who's made of the same
"You fall in a minute"
Said the twin to your flame

> **Write a piece about**
>
> The guy who introduced me to your music and then ghosted me two months later

Facepalm
Keke Palmer pop quiz
I'm sorry
I'm sorry
I don't know who that man is

Write a piece about
Air

I'm allergic to turtlenecks
Allergic to titles
And allergic to taking things fast
So please don't jump the gun
And tell me you love me
Cuz I might answer
"I don't think I asked"
I need to breathe
I need some air
I need space like I'm half of the moon
Blame it on trauma
Or blame it on karma
Or blame it on crowning in June

Write a piece about

Big butts

I felt like a lily
leaning into the sun
BUT should've known
I was just leaning into the gun
I could love him
BUT he disappears on the weekends
I could love him
BUT he seems scared of the deep end
I could love him
BUT he still seeks outside validation
I could love him
BUT there's no reciprocation
BBL baby
The BUT is obese
Baby-boys
Broken . . .
Leave me in peace

Write a piece about

Serenity

I have realized
that there's a very real possibility
that serenity is overrated
You know why Hallmark movies suck?
And why kid shows get boring the more you grow up?
Because something in you
Deep down
Looks for tension
'Cause a walk in the park is a walk in the park
but it's boring the tenth time over
But a walk in the dark—
A walk in the dark is a movie

Write a piece about

Grief II

Mortal love
The great defect
That leaves what was
drowned deep in debt
It was only real
If hard to forget
Grief is the desert
the ocean left

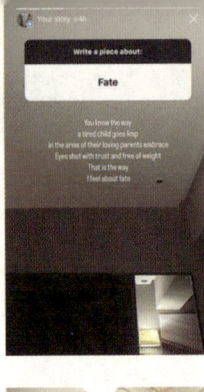
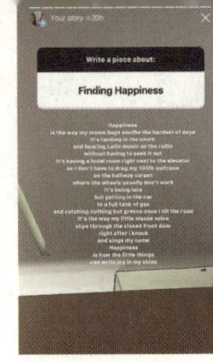

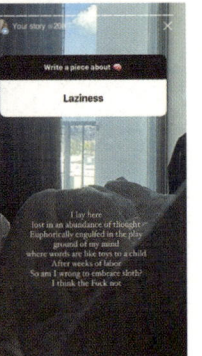
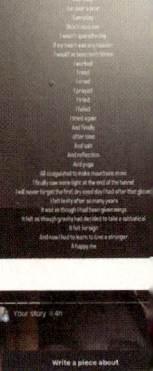

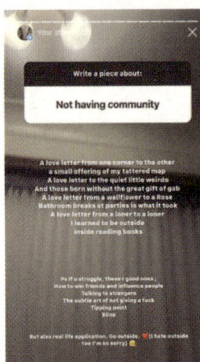
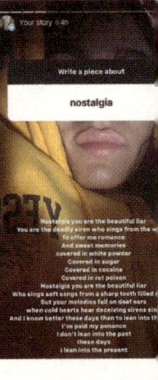
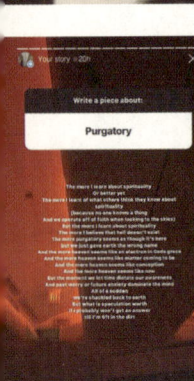

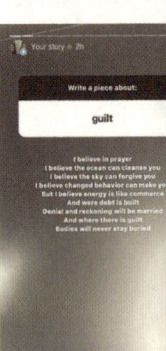

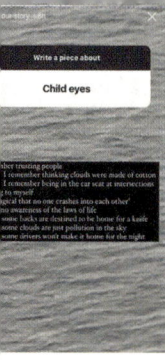
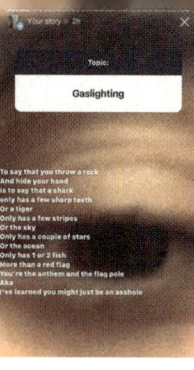
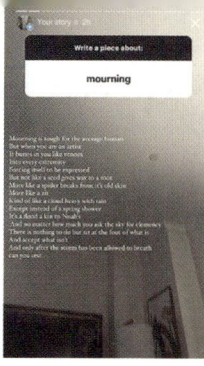

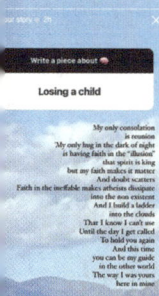

Life

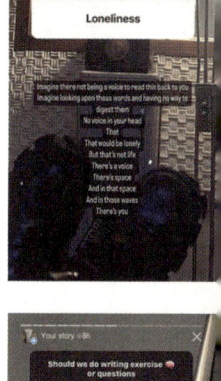
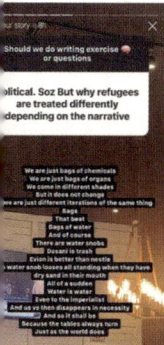
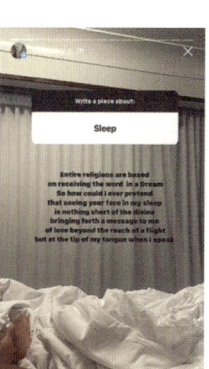

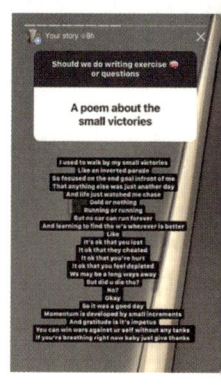
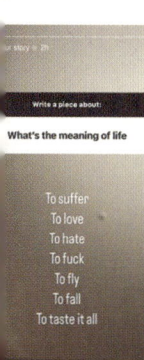
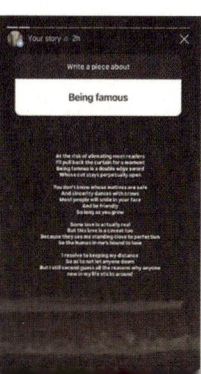

Write a piece about

The meaning of life

To suffer
To love
To hate
To fuck
To fly
To fall
To taste it all

Write a piece about

Mourning

Mourning is tough for the average human
But when you are an artist
It bursts in you like venom
Into every extremity
Forcing itself to be expressed
But not like a seed gives way to a root
More like a snake breaks from its old skin
More like a zit
Kind of like a cloud heavy with rain
Except instead of a spring shower
It's a flood akin to Noah's
And no matter how much you ask the sky for clemency
There is nothing to do but sit at the foot of what is
And accept what isn't
And only after the storm has been allowed to breathe

can you rest in the morning

Write a piece about

Not having community

A love letter from one corner to the other
A small offering of my tattered map
A love letter to the quiet little weirdo
And those born without the great gift of gab
A love letter from a wallflower to a rose
Bathroom breaks at parties is really what it took
A love letter from a loner to a loner
I learned to be outside
inside reading books

PS if u struggle, these r good ones:
How to Win Friends and Influence People
Talking to Strangers
The Subtle Art of Not Giving a F*c*k
The Tipping Point
Blink
But also real-life application: Go outside.
(I hate outside too I'm so sorry)

Write a piece about

Child eyes

I remember trusting people
Just like I remember thinking clouds were made of cotton
Just like I remember being in the car seat at intersections
thinking to myself
"How magical that no one crashes into each other"
Having no awareness of the laws of life
Or that some backs are destined to be home for a knife
Or that some clouds are just pollution in the sky
Or that some drivers won't make it home for the night

Write a piece about

Gaslighting

To say that you throw a rock
And hide your hand
Is to say that a shark
Only has a few sharp teeth
Or a tiger
Only has a few stripes
Or the sky
Only has a couple of stars
Or the ocean
Only a couple of fish
More than a red flag
You're the anthem and the phallic flagpole
A.K.A.
I've learned you might just be an asshole

Write a piece about

Control

Fighting for the wheel
To correct to the right
When the road's veering left
is like taunting God's might

Control is a myth
The devil's an opp
Sometimes it's just best
to let go and let God

Write a piece about

Father-daughter love

When I was little
My dad moved us out to the suburbs
Like most children, I was blind to nuance
I just wanted to stay put with my friends in Driftwood
But this was a better area
With safer schools, and more space, and a bigger room
But sadly a lot less color
I remember some kids getting this silver-rubber-wheeled Razor scooter
I remember begging for it but being told it was too expensive
I remember being disappointed
But I don't remember being perceived
A few days later
I got home and found my dad in the garage
Next to him, he had a few pieces of spare wood
(which he had swiped from work)
Some paint cans and some worn-in black wheels
A few hours later, the magician was done
Voilà
There in front of him
was my new wooden scooter
Painted in Colombia colors
I think I half smiled
How insane
How insane it was to have paid for a million-dollar memory
with a half smile
Thankfully, the years have seen my smile grow along with me
And appreciation seeps out through my eyes when I think back
When I think of him
The word *love* doesn't do this memory justice
Mi papi
My dad
My magician

Write a piece about

Tranquility

12:00 a.m.
Sleep escapes
I am the only one awake
We've just moved from the city to the suburbs
I miss Driftwood and my old school and my brother
I get out of bed
Bare feet on the floor
I stand by my parents' open bedroom door
I watch my father's chest rise and fall
Rise and fall
to verify
And give me peace
That it's only sleep
Then I check my mother's
Then I check the locks
Then I check the windows
I see lonely trees
and an empty street
Turtles move faster than these midnight minutes
I hear nothing but crickets
Crickets I used to complain about
because I missed the sirens
Funny how anxiety and tranquility are cousins

Write a piece about

The unknown infinite vastness of the universe

We barely know the recipe to reality
We have the slightest grip on sexuality
and know nothing of immortality
Yet paintings and scriptures from God's mind
(through the filter of the hand of man)
are glorified
We claim to know the rules
And claim to know the limits
And claim to know the world's modality
We claim that the pattern is duality
But if that is so
And I were to spit on gravity
And start to float
Rise up to heaven
And sit on a cloud of smoke
Would you call me a witch?
Would you call it insanity?
If I were to bend rules you thought were made of steel
Using my thought alone
Would you call me a god?
Or would you call it blasphemy?
I respect faith
when it is called by its name
But to say you know the universe
Is to say God's name in vain

Write a piece about

Fate

You know the way
a tired child goes limp
in the arms of their loving parent's embrace
Eyes shut with trust and free of all weight
That's how I feel about fate

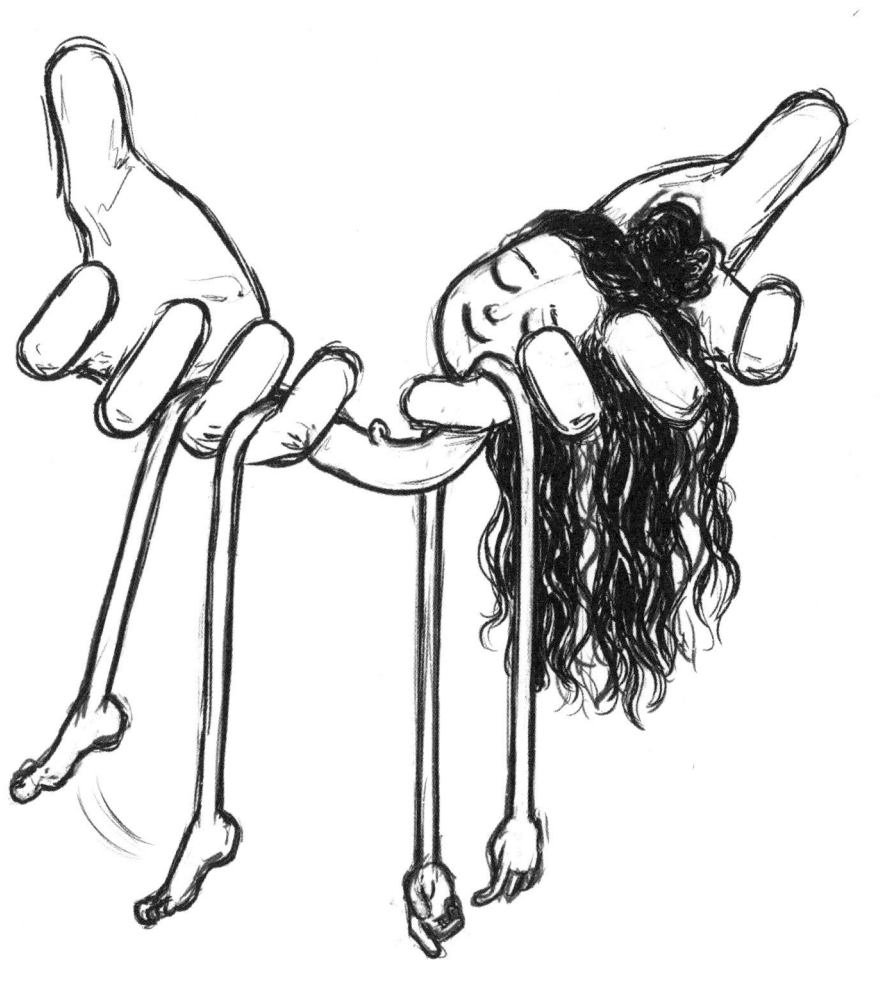

Write a piece about

An untouched river in the jungle

If I could exchange my limbs
for branches of a tree
And be carried by the water
forever
I'd be free
If I could exchange my heart
For a simple fallen leaf
And be carried by the water
forever
I'd be free
Joy would fill my spirit
And my smile would never leave
If I was carried by the water
forever
I would be free

Write a piece about

Finding happiness

Happiness
Is the way my mom's hug soothes the hardest of days
It's landing in the South
and hearing cumbia on the radio
without having to seek it out
It's having a hotel room right next to the elevator
And not having to lug my thousand-pound suitcase down an
endless
carpeted
hallway
It's being late
but getting in the car
to a full tank of gas
and catching nothing but greens once I hit the road
It's the way my little niece's voice
slips through the front door
when she sings my name
right after I've knocked
Joy

Write a piece about

Free Palestine

If I cry for strangers
I can't imagine the pools of tears their families must harbor
I can't imagine the fields of purple Faqqua iris
that their tears could water
If I pray for strangers
I can't imagine the supplications to heaven
from the mothers of those who have fallen
I can't imagine the volume of hymns asking God
for a land that is sovereign
And though the empathy in my heart might render me defeated
That is not my emotion to bear
For I have been gifted the guilt of a spectator
By the dice of destiny, I happen to not be on the receiving end
And though I might feel useless on the opposite side of a screen,
If all I can do is amplify
and make sure the walls of time have the story right,
then I will
And history will bear witness
Just like Voltaire's haunting truth:
"Every man is guilty of all the good he did not do"

Write a piece about

Your life

I was in the airport
Running and late as usual
When the emergency lights came on
"Find cover, get away from the windows,
find cover, get away from the windows"
I look to my right and see a hurricane outside
It's approaching
My assistant and I run for cover
She is six feet to my left
The wrath of God is twenty feet to my right
With the ease of a giant plucking petals apart,
the winds lift the steel roof above us
tear the flooring from the ground
and rip people into the sky
The black funnel nears
Fifteen feet
Ten feet
Death is imminent
Five feet
I feel urgency
but not fear
I look to my left,
I try to give her warning and share my love and well-wishes
into the next life,
but it's too late
And she's too far
So I concede to my final seconds of life
And find refuge in memories
I think of my family
Of the ones I love the most
I see their faces and in MILLIseconds

I feel the sweetness of a life well-lived
They fade
I breathe
I prepare for the end
I don't resist
I let God's destiny end my carnal shift here
I see smoke
I close my eyes and see gray
I feel cold
I wait for pain but feel none
I think I've crossed over
Then I see patterns
I see the rings of life circling the trunk of a tree
Spirit's floating
I coach myself to stay serene and continue to reject fear
My eyes are still closed
"Open them. Don't be afraid."
I wake up on my flight
Heading to Perth
In the sky
But
Living in the sky

Write a piece about
Guilt

I believe in prayer
I believe the ocean can cleanse you
I believe the sky can forgive you
And I believe changed behavior can make you
But I believe energy is like commerce
And where debt is built
Denial and reckoning will be married
And where there is guilt
Bodies will never stay buried

Write a piece about

Geminis

Well,
Hell.
—fin

> **Write a piece about**
>
> **Staying quiet when someone insults you**

I once knew a soul
who was as calm as a pond
I've always been a hurricane
So his peace used to leave me perplexed
Until one day
I watched the devil dance by the pond
I watched the devil throw embers at the calm
But the tranquil remained unperturbed and still stayed still
Then the wind took one of the embers and carried it to my skin
by chance
Hot went my wick
And my storm ensued
My reaction caught the devil's eye
He laughed and danced over to me
Bored with the calm
And amused at my riot
He took more embers and sprinkled them on my flesh
I cursed
His eyes widened and he laughed again
Another ember on my tongue
It lashed him
He laughed again
He found rhythm
This pattern continued until numbness took me over
Finally silence landed
We sat and stared at each other for hours
but eventually the red one grew bored
When the devil went away
I turned and noticed that the calm one had stayed
He whispered
"When you engage with evil
You invite it to play"

Write a piece about

Looking into someone's eyes and feeling peace and happiness

I pray for death before you
Because I only know peace with you
And Earth will be just a rock
And the sun just a flame
And the sky just a club I can't get into
If God doesn't hear me
Earth without you should fear me
For I will spit in the face of life
And I will not know peace again
I will just be dying slowly
Waiting until I can ascend

Write a piece about

Loneliness

Imagine there not being a voice to read this back to you
Imagine looking upon these words
And having no way to
digest them
No voice in your head
That
That would be lonely
But that's not life
There's a voice
There's a space
And in that space
And in those waves
There's you

Write a piece about

Nostalgia

Nostalgia
You are the beautiful liar
You are the deadly siren who sings from the water
To offer me romance
And sweet memories
Covered in white powder
Covered in sugar
Covered in cocaine
Covered in rat poison
Nostalgia
You are the beautiful liar
With an ugly heart
Who wears too much makeup
And who sings soft songs from a sharp tooth-filled mouth
But I've ripped my ears from my head
And the fountain of blood their absence bore
Morphed into a red river
That my heart has used to travel north

Write a piece about

Losing a child

My only consolation
is reunion
My only hug in the dark of night
is having faith in the "illusion"
that spirit is king
But my faith makes it matter
And doubt scatters
Faith in the ineffable
makes atheists dissipate
into the nonexistent
And I build a ladder
into the clouds
That I know I can't use
Until the day I get called
To hold you again
And this time
you can be my guide
in the other world
The way I was yours
here in mine

Write a piece about

Mothers

To speak of my mother
Is to speak of a bed after a ten-hour shift
To speak of her
Is to speak of a warm jacket in the Arctic tundra
To speak of her
Is to speak of a hug to the lonely
My mother
The saint
The mother to all
Guilty of a heart too big to be held by societal norms
The indiscriminate hugger
My bridge to spirit
And home to the greatest love I've ever known
Mi mejor amiga
Mi madre linda

Write a piece about

Dreaming you're back in high school again

I think it was God's gift to you
that I didn't blossom in my conviction until my twenties
I've always had the bullets loaded
but I lacked the fervor of a trigger-happy woman
In my youth I had more diplomacy
And more consideration for another's emotional life
But one can only have so much patience
Piles of bodies no longer make me wince
I still have prudence when I share truth with the kind and sensitive
But the years have taught me to meet fire with flame
And some nights
I dream of turning you into ashes

Write a piece about

Purgatory

The more I learn about spirituality
Or better yet
The more I learn of what others think they know about spirituality
The more I believe that hell doesn't exist
The more purgatory seems as though it's here
but we just gave earth the wrong name
And the more heaven seems like an electron in God's grace
And the more heaven seems like matter coming to be
And the more heaven seems like conception
And the more heaven seems like "the now"
But the moment we let time dictate our awareness
And past worry or future anxiety dominate the mind
All of a sudden
we're shackled back to earth
Anyway
what is speculation worth?
If I probably won't get an answer
till I'm six feet in the dirt

Write a piece about

Politics. Sucks but why refugees are treated differently depending on the narrative

We are just bags of chemical reactions
We are just bags of organs
We come in different shades
But it does not change
That we are just different iterations of the same
Bags
That beat
Bags of water
And of course
There are water snobs
But a water snob
loses all standing
when they have dry sand in their mouth
All of a sudden
Water is water
Even to the imperialist
And *us vs. them* disappears in necessity
And we might just live to see it
Because the tables always turn
Just as the world does

Write a piece about

Sleep

Entire religions
are based on
receiving God's word in a dream
So how could I not
deem it sacred
when it's your face I see in my sleep?

Write a piece about

Small victories

I used to walk by my small victories
carelessly
Like an inverted parade
So focused on the end goal in front of me
that anything else was just another day
And life just watched me chase away
Gold or nothing
Running or running
But there's not a car in the world that can run forever
Mining love in the L's of the minutia is better

Write a piece about

Laziness

I lay here
lost in an abundance of thought
Euphorically engulfed in the playground of my mind
where words are like toys to a child
after weeks of labor
So am I wrong to embrace sloth?
I think the fuck not

Write a piece about

Space

I love catching afternoon flights
when the plane breaches just above the clouds
as the sun is setting
And the vastness is illuminated with a pink dusk
In those moments I'm reminded,
I'm closer to God than I am man
And space is everywhere
And the sun is always shining somewhere
And the moon is always up somewhere
And I'm reminded that in reality everything exists all at once

Write a piece about

The news

In a quest to be informed
Why am I left more confused
Why am I being fed darkness
As if the goal is to be amused
Years ago my old Mary Jane
once took me on a flight
And I made the sad mistake
Of watching my TV screen all night
And racism and fear
And politics and traffic
painted pictures of the world
And painted everything as tragic
But if the mind creates your life
And if these waves affect my thoughts
Is it masochistic to watch the news?
Instead should I read some Alan Watts?
Maybe
It would serve us more
To decide to watch ourselves
And the news just might get better
If the mirror were to get some help

Write a piece about

People watching on the subway platform

I love being on a train
And locking eyes with someone who's waiting for the next one
I love diving into them for all of those four seconds
I love their initial reluctance to slow dance in my gaze
The first second is fear
My smile comes in the second second
And in the third
I feel them relax
The apple of their cheek rises up
By the most imperceptible millimeter
Then in the last second
They're mine
We find connection
Fearlessly
Unencumbered by commitment
Because I'll never see them again
But I've seen their soul
And they've slow danced with mine
And just like that
We smile our goodbyes

Write a piece about

Moving through fear

Tania Peralta once wrote
"If I am scared
it means I have to do it"
And it hit my soul
like sunlight to a flower
And it hit my heart
like a dart to a bullseye
And it resonated in my entire body
Like the bass makes your body shake
at the very front of the stage
And I loved it
And I love it
Because my favorite thing to say
at the foot of fear
is "fuck it"

Write a piece about

Being famous

At the risk of alienating most readers
I'll pull back the curtain for a bit
Being famous is a double-edged sword
Whose inflicted wounds stay perpetually slit
I don't know whose motives are safe
And sincerity dances with crows
Most people will smile in my face and be friendly
Contingent on the assumption that my caché grows
Some love is actually real
But this love has a caveat too
Because they place me on a pedestal of pompous perfection
Where the human in me's bound to lose
So I resolve to keeping my distance
So as to not let anyone down
And I still second-guess all the reasons why anyone new in my life sticks around

Write a piece about

Realizing you wasted your youth

No sir
I rebuke it
No sir
I wholly refuse
to subscribe to the idea
of realizing wasted youth
Fuck that shallow fable
My truth is more profound
You will never be as young
As your "old ass" is right now

Write a piece about

Rivers

Like a redemption song to a killer
Like weightlessness to a rock
Like holy water to a sinner
Rivers give me everything I am not

Write a piece about

Finally being able to feel happiness after years

You might not believe me
But there was a time
I cried
every day
for over a year
Every
day
Didn't miss one
I wasn't spared a day
If my heart was any heavier, I would've been immobile
But I worked
I read
I cried
I prayed
I tried
I failed
I tried again
And finally
after time
And salt
And reflection
And yoga
All my endeavors and efforts coagulated enough to stop the bleeding
And I finally saw some light at the end of the tunnel
I will never forget the first dry-eyed day I had after that gloom
It was as though I had been given wings

And then I had to learn to love a new stranger in my house
A girl I didn't really know
A *happy* me

Write a piece about

Stubbing your toe on the table when you were having a good day

I was saved by the heavens from the hand of a man
Once I healed, my heart leaped back to earth
But my peace was short lived like a kingdom of sand
Because I landed and broke my neck in the dirt
Mary Magdalene swam in the river of God
But I am committed to drown in merlot
Gabriel gave me clouds on which my poor feet could walk
But I am committed to stubbing my toe

Write a piece about

Financial struggles

You have to read *Rich Dad Poor Dad*
Tony Robbins *Unshakeable* too
If all you've been doing is working to save
It won't be enough for the needle to move
It's been said it takes money to make money
You must learn to make debt your friend
Throw bands if it's an investment
So long as it's a means to an end
Learn to recognize an asset
And aim to be your own boss
Time is the only real currency
And the goal's to spend it doing what you love

Write a piece about

Missing someone too much

I used to feel like I needed to take a breath
before holding your gaze
because I wasn't equipped to travel into the galaxies of your eyes
As if I needed an anchor to hold me to earth

Strokes of green, hints of yellow and pretty drops of blue
It's been years since we've talked
Yet I still think of you

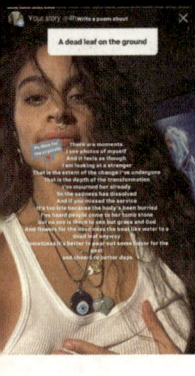
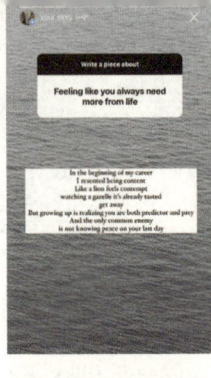
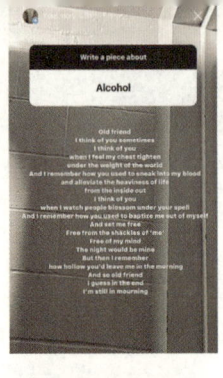
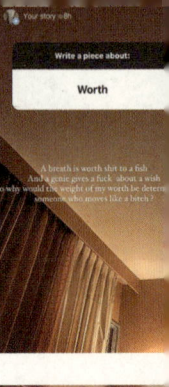
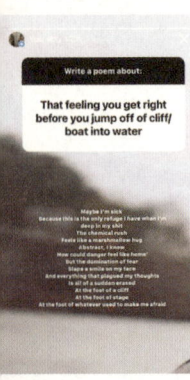
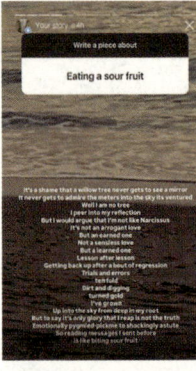
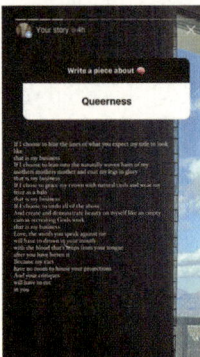

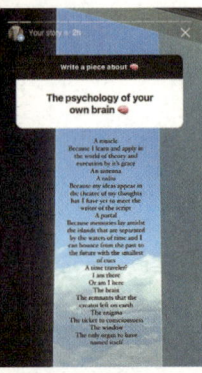
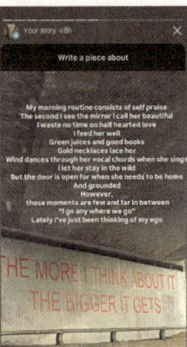

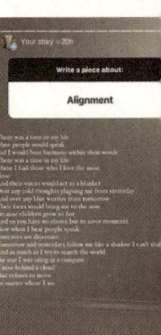
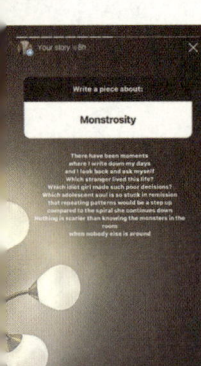
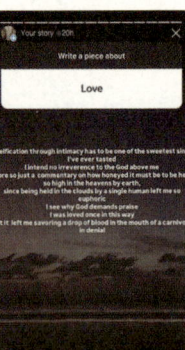
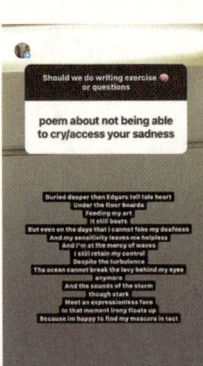
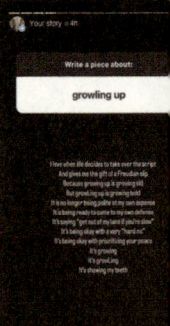

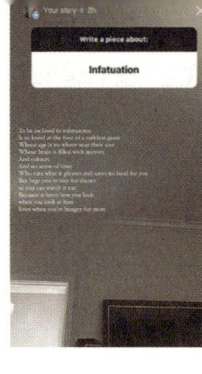
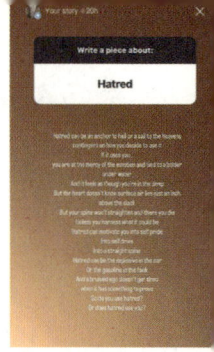
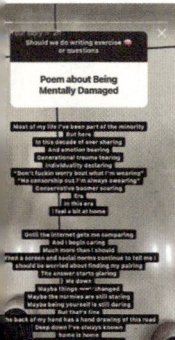

Mental Health

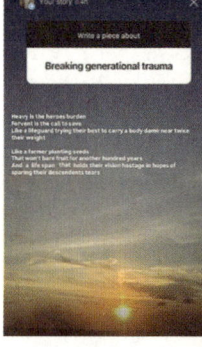
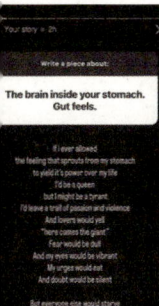
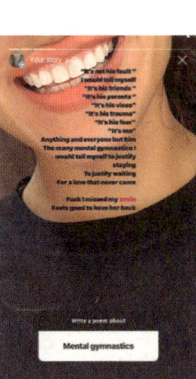

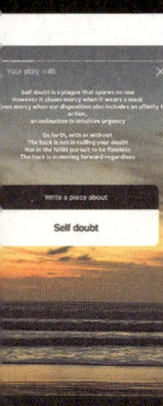
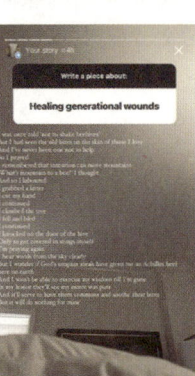

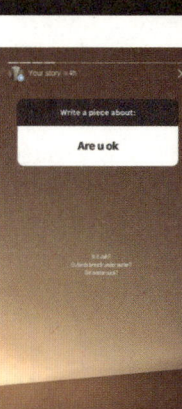

Write a piece about

A dead leaf on the ground

There are moments
I see photos of myself
And it feels as though
I am looking at a stranger
That is the extent of the change I've undergone
That is the depth of the transformation
I've mourned her already
So the sadness has dissolved
And if you missed the service
It's too late because the body's been buried
I've heard people come to her tombstone
But they only find grass and God
And flowers for the dead miss the mark
like water to a dead leaf anyway

> **Write a piece about**
>
> Graffiti on the side of the highway:
> "The more I think about it, the bigger it gets"

My morning routine consists of self-praise
The second I see the mirror I call her beautiful
I waste no time on half-hearted love
I feed her well
Green juices and good books
Gold necklaces lace her
Wind dances through her vocal cords when she sings
I let her stay in the wild
But the door is open for when she needs to be home
And grounded
However,
those moments are few and far between
"I go anywhere we go"
Lately I've just been giving boujee roses to my ego

Write a piece about

Your mental state atm

I am a seed in the wind
Free of any man's plan but that of God's ambition
I am the dreamer and I am the dream
I am the watcher and I am the seen
I am the creator and the created
And the demolished and all in between

I am love
And I am fury
And I am
I am
I am
I move any mountain in front of me
Because spirit said I can

Write a piece about

Whether or not you're OK

Is it July?
Do birds breathe underwater?
Did *Avatar* suck?

(It's January)

Write a piece about

Being mentally damaged

Most of my life I've been part of the minority
But here
In this decade of
Oversharing
Emotional baring and emotional bearing
Generational trauma tearing
Individuality declaring
"Don't fuckin' worry 'bout what I'm wearing"
"No censorship cuz I'm always swearing"
Conservative boomer scaring
—era
In this era
I feel a bit at home
Until the internet gets me comparing
And I begin caring
Much more than I should
When a screen and social norms continue to tell me
I should be worried about finding my pairing
The answer starts glaring
Me down
Maybe things haven't changed
Maybe the normies are still staring
Maybe being yourself is still daring
But that's fine
The back of my hand has a hand-drawing of this road
Deep down I've always known
home is home
Regardless of if I'm home alone

Write a piece about

Alcohol

Old friend
I think of you sometimes
I think of you
when I feel my chest tighten
under the weight of the world
And I remember how you used to sneak into my blood
and alleviate the heaviness of life
from the inside out
I think of you
when I watch people blossom under your spell
And I remember how you used to baptize me out of myself
And set me free
Free from the shackles of "me"
Free of my mind
The night would be mine
But then I remember
how hollow you'd leave me in the morning
So instead I just sit and longingly watch
As others soothe their sorrows
Feasting from the fruit I've been forbidden to touch

Write a piece about

Queerness

If I choose to blur the lines of what you expect my title to look like
that is my business
If I choose to lean into the naturally woven hairs
of my mother's mother's mother
and coat my legs in glory
that is my business
If I choose to grace my crown with natural curls
and wear my frizz as a halo
that is my business
If I choose to undo all of the above
And create and demonstrate beauty on myself
like an empty canvas
synthetically re-creating God's work
that is my business
The words you speak against me will have to drown in your mouth
with the blood that seeps from your tongue
after you have bitten it
Because my ears
have no room to house your projections
And your critiques
will have to rot
in you

Write a piece about

Hatred

Hatred can be an anchor to hell or a sail to the heavens
contingent on how you decide to use it
If it uses you,
you are at the mercy of emotion and tied to a boulder
underwater
It may feel as though you're in the deep
But the heart doesn't know surface air lies just an inch
above the slack
Sadly, your spine won't straighten
So there you die
Unless you harness what it could be
Hatred can motivate you into self-pride
Into self-drive
Into a straight spine
Hatred can be the explosive in the car
Or the gasoline in the tank
And a bruised ego doesn't get tired when it has something to prove
So do you use hatred?
Or does hatred use you?

> **Write a piece about**
>
> **Hope**

I read somewhere that
"hope dies last"
And it crushed me
like a dandelion in the eye of a gardener

Not dead yet
But soon to be

Write a piece about

Monstrosity

There have been moments
when I write down my days
Just to look back and ask myself
Which stranger lived this?
Which idiot girl made such poor decisions?
Which adolescent soul is so stuck in remission
that repeating patterns would be a step up
compared to the spiral she continues down?
Do you know what you would do
if you'd spent years trying to kill the monster
just to realize
after all those nights
the monster had been you?

Write a piece about

Not being able to cry or access your sadness

Buried much deeper
Than Mr. Poe's Tell-Tale Heart
Under the floorboards
Feeding scraps to my art
Denying all weakness
The tears have been trapped
Though my chest might be bleeding
My mascara's intact

Write a piece about

Mental gymnastics

"It's not his fault"
I would tell myself
"It's his friends"
"It's his parents"
"It's his vices"
"It's his trauma"
"It's his fear"
"It's me"
Anything and everyone but him
The many mental gymnastics
I would tell myself to justify staying
To justify waiting
For a love that never came
Fuck I missed my smile
Feels good to have her back

Write a piece about

Eating a sour fruit

From way up in the azure
I reached down into my root
And found a buried truth
that my past could not refute
An emo pygmied pick-me
Grown too shockingly astute
Seeing how far I've come is akin to biting sour fruit

> **Write a piece about**
>
> **That feeling you get right before you jump off of a cliff/boat into water**

Maybe I'm sick
But it feels like a gift
When my pupils go wide
And my gravity lifts
Abstract, I know
That danger is home
But dominion of fear
Leads where I need to go
Into the dark
Without slowing my pace
Because to hesitate here
Would make me a slave
At the foot of a cliff
At the foot of a stage

At the foot of whatever used to make me afraid

Write a piece about

The "avoidant" attachment

I'm sick
Send help

Write a piece about

The psychology of your own brain

A muscle
Because I learn in the world of theory
But execute to full physical fruition by its grace
A radio
Because my ideas appear in the theater of my thoughts
but I have yet to meet the writer of the script
A portal
Because memories live on islands separated by the waters of time
But I skip from shore to shore
From past to future
with the smallest of cues
Home of the great grey matter
The folded enigma
The ticket to consciousness
The window to God
And the only organ
to have named itself

> **Write a piece about**
>
> The brain inside your stomach. Gut feels.

If I were to ever allow
the feeling that sprouts from my stomach
to yield its power over my life
I'd be a queen
but I'd be a tyrant
I'd leave a trail of passion and violence
And lovers would yell
"Here comes the giant"
My eyes would be vibrant
And all fear would sleep
All doubts would be silent
And my urges would eat
But everyone else would starve

Write a piece about

Alignment

There was a time in my life
when I had those who I love the most
Close
And I would hear harmony in their words
And their voices would act as a blanket
over any cold thoughts plaguing me from yesterday
and over any blue worries from tomorrow
Their faces would bring me to the now
Because children grow fast
So you have no choice but to savor moments
But now
I'm in a place where sentences are dissonant
Tomorrows and yesterdays follow me like shades I can't flee
And as much as I try to search the world
the star I was using as a compass
is now behind a cloud
that refuses to move
no matter where I am
The harmony is off
And the blanket is gone

Write a piece about

Witchy women being burned at the stake

Flames of fire at my feet
But I find no fear inside
Hail mother Mary I'm dying free
My mind is mine though my hands are tied

Write a piece about

Breaking generational trauma

Heavy is the hero's burden
Fervent is the call to save
Like a lifeguard trying their best to carry
a body damn near twice their weight
But I make calls and I swallow pride
Trying to spare my young one's tears
Like a farmer planting baby seeds
That won't bear fruit for a hundred years

Write a piece about

Healing generational wounds

I was once told "not to shake beehives"
But bites on the skin of those I loved silently begged for a broker
For a fearless interceder
And at the risk of sounding sanctimonious
I've never been one to not help
At first I held my inclination to action at bay
And instead I prayed
I willingly turned a blind eye to the road to hell
And instead remembered that intention can move mountains
"What's a mountain to a bee?" I thought
So I labored
I grabbed the ladder
I cut my hand
I continued
I climbed the tree
I fell and bled
I continued
When I finally arrived
I knocked on the door of the hive
Only to get covered in stings myself
I'm praying again
I hear words from the sky clearly
But I wonder if God's utopian ideals
have given me an Achilles' heel here on earth
And I won't be able to exercise my wisdom till I'm gone
Everyone loves the dead
So in my honor they'll finally see my intent was pure
Maybe they'll knock on a hive themselves
Maybe memories of me will serve to have them commune
And reunions will soothe their bites
Sadly they'll do nothing for mine

Along with tears in their eyes
I hope they're gifted vision
And empathy
Instead of asking
"Why is she crying
like she's the victim?"

Write a piece about

A grassy field

I take a deep breath
Drop my heavy bag
My shoulders smile
I take my hoodie off
The sun touches my skin
and whispers "I missed you"
The breeze gives me goosebumps
It whispers "I missed you too"
I take my Converse off
Socks set my feet free
My toes greet the grass
And stretch out
as if to say good morning
I sit
into my own little corner of this world
In front of me runs a river
Behind me a forest feeds the air
And inside
I am calm

Write a piece about

Grounding

Blades of blessed green grass
A conduit for my stress to pass
A bed at the end of my tired path
A soothing song to my human wrath

Write a piece about
Self-doubt

Go forth, with or without
The hack is not in culling your doubt
Nor in the futile pursuit to be flawless
The hack is in moving forward regardless

> **Write a piece about**
>
> **Feeling like you always need more from life**

In the beginning of my career
I resented being content
Like a lion feels contempt
watching a gazelle it's already tasted
get away
But growing up is realizing you are both predator and prey
And the only common enemy
is not knowing peace on your last day

Write a piece about

Growling up

I love when life decides to take over the script
And gives me the gift of a Freudian slip
Because growing up is growing old
But growLing up is growing bold
It's no longer being polite at my own expense
It's being ready to come to my own defense
It's saying "get out of my lane if you're slow"
It's being OK with a very hard "no"
It's being OK with prioritizing my peace
It's growing
It's growLing
It's showing my teeth

Write a piece about

Standing your ground

Trying to exercise self-worth
used to hurt
when I used to think
that I'd miss out
unless I was kind
inevitably
and imperviously
regardless of whether the situation or person deserved it or not

But time changes you
In my past I've been guilty of saying
"It costs nothing to be nice"
But it does
It charges you pieces of your character
Every time you betray yourself
for the sake of someone else's comfort
With the power of God
never again will I chase shit
And I will always let things be
Because no one in the world
can take away what's ultimately meant for me

Write a piece about
Worth

A breath is worth shit to a fish
And a genie gives a fuck about a wish
So why would the weight of my worth be determined
by someone who moves like a bitch?

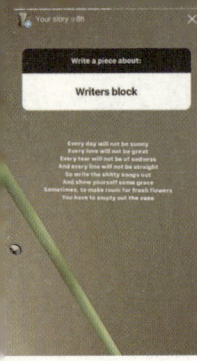
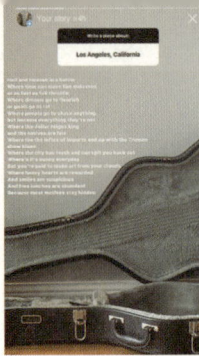
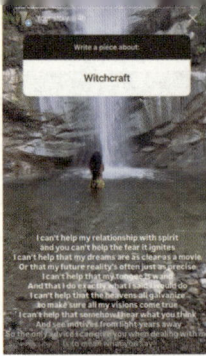

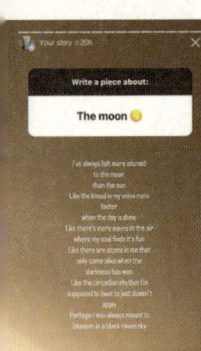
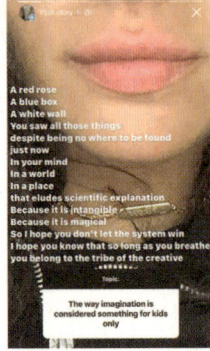
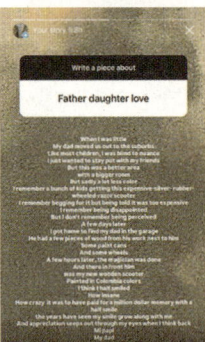
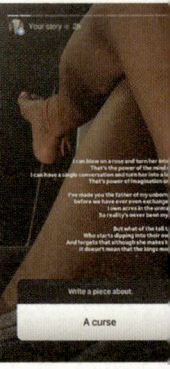
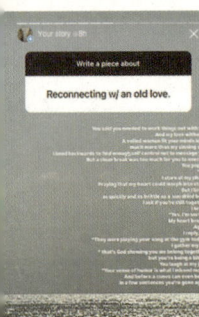

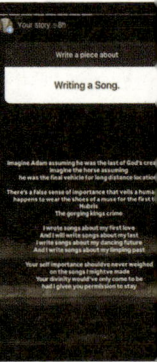
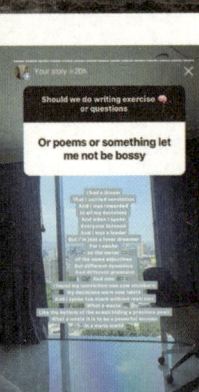
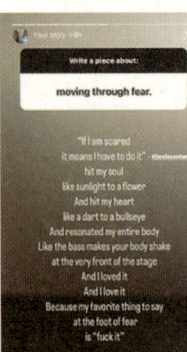
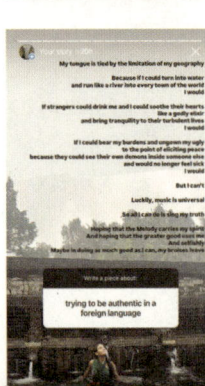
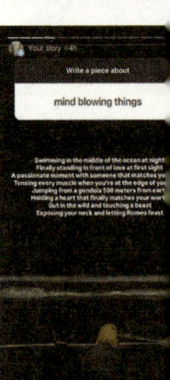

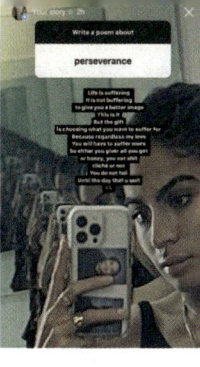
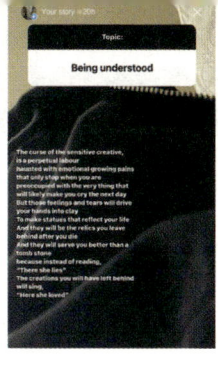
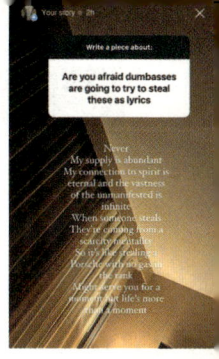

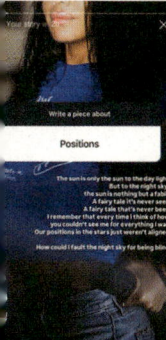

Creativity

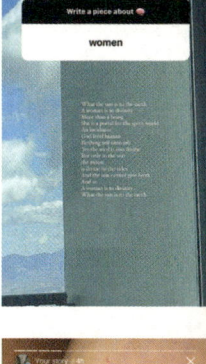

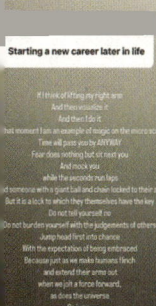

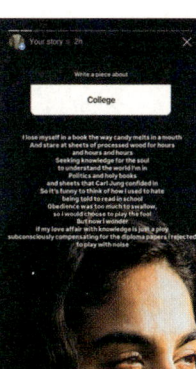
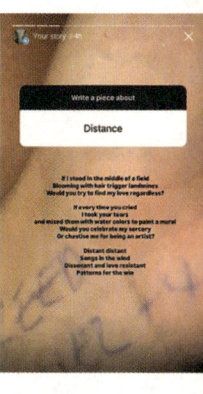

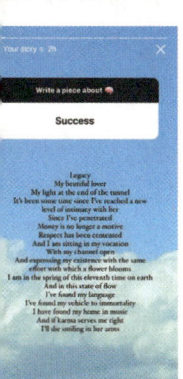
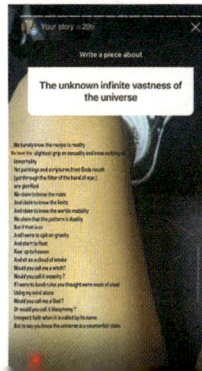

Write a piece about

The moon

I've always felt more attuned
to the moon
than the sun
Like the blood in my veins runs
faster
when the day is done
Like there are more waves in the air
and my soul
finds its fun
Like there are atoms in me
that only come alive
when darkness has won
Like the circadian rhythm most beat to
just doesn't apply
Perhaps I was always meant to blossom
in a black raven sky

Write a piece about

Writer's block

Every day will not be sunny
Every love will not be great
Every tear will not be of sadness
And every line will not be straight
So write the shitty songs out,
Show yourself some grace
To make room for fresh flowers
You have to empty out the vase

> **Write a piece about**
>
> Are you afraid dumbasses are going to try to steal these to use as lyrics?

Never
My supply is abundant
My connection to spirit is eternal
and the vastness of the unmanifested is infinite
When someone steals
they suffer from a sleeping wisdom and forget their gift
It's like stealing a Lexus with no gas in the tank
While you have a garage full of Lambos

> **Write a piece about**
>
> **A curse**

I can blow on a rose and turn her into a jungle
That's the power of the mind untamed
I can have a single conversation and turn her into a love story
That's the power of imagination unmaimed
I've made you the father of my unborn children
before I have ever even touched your skin
I own acres in the fields of the budding nascent
So reality catches up to what I decide to begin
But what of the tall tale-teller
Who starts dipping into her own supply
And forgets that although she makes kingdoms
It doesn't mean that the king's men comply

Write a piece about

Distance

If every time you cried
I took your tears
And mixed them with watercolors to paint a mural
Would you celebrate my sorcery
Or chastise me for being an artist?

Distant distant
Songs in the wind
Dissonant and love-resistant
Patterns for the win

Write a piece about

Being understood

The curse of the sensitive creative
is a perpetual labor
haunted with emotional growing pains
that only stop
when you are preoccupied
with the very thing
that will likely make you cry the next day
But those feelings and tears drive your hands into clay
To make statues that reflect your life
And they will be the relics you leave behind after you die
And they will serve you better than a tombstone
And better than anyone's eulogy
because instead of reading
"Here she lies"
The creations you will have left behind
will sing,
"Here she loved"

Write a piece about

Perseverance

Life is suffering
It is not buffering
to give you a better image
This is it
But the gift
is choosing what you want to suffer for
Because regardless
you will have to suffer more

Either you give 'er all you got
Or prepare to eat some shit
Cliché or not, you do not fail
Until the day you quit

Write a piece about

Los Angeles, California

Blue-skied California
And red flames in a bottle
Where time can move like molasses
or as fast as full fuckin' throttle
Where dreams can go to flourish
or goals will go to rot
Where people chase potential
but become everything they're not

Where the golden buck is king
and the natives are shockingly few
Where the influx of imports
All get a case of the *Truman Show* blues
Where the city somehow grew teeth
and the parties can spit you back out
Where it's normal that it's sunny every day
But the artists make art from their clouds

> **Write a piece about**
>
> **Spirit animals**

I've met animals
who make me safe havens
Who make entire worlds
with motivational quotes written on padded walls
Who wipe tears from my eyes
Who hold space for my pain
and validate my illogical world of emotions
Who tell me of God
And tell me of love
And tell me of peace
without a single word
And without a single movement
Without doing anything but being

Write a piece about

Success

Legacy
My beautiful lover
My light at the end of the tunnel
It's been some time since I've reached a new level of intimacy with her
Since I've penetrated
Money is no longer a motive
Amen
Respect has been cemented
Amen
And I am sitting in my vocation
With my channel open
And expressing my existence
With the same effort
With which a flower blooms
I am in the spring of this eleventh hour on earth
And in this state of flow
I've found my language
I have found my vehicle to immortality
I have found my home in art

If karma serves me right
I'll die smiling in her arms

Write a piece about

The way imagination is considered something for kids only

A red rose
A blue box
A white wall
You saw all those things
despite being nowhere to be found
just now
In your mind
In a world
In a place that eludes scientific explanation
Because it is intangible
Because it is magical
So I hope you don't let the system win
I hope you know that so long as you breathe,
you belong to the commune of the creative

Write a piece about

The feeling when you write

Watching someone articulate their emotions
in a conversation pertinent to what they are
currently feeling
smoothly
Is like watching someone walk
while I barely stay up on crutches
It's like watching someone swim
while I sit on the edge of the shallow end
with a life jacket duct-taped to my body

But writing my feelings
Is like watching a formerly caged bird fly
after being gifted its freedom

> **Write a piece about**
>
> Poems or something? Let me not be bossy

I had a dream
That I carried conviction
And I was rewarded
In all my decisions
And when I spoke
Everyone listened
And I was a leader
But I'm just a fever dreamer
For I awoke
as the owner
of the same adjectives
But different dynamics
And different pronouns
And now
I find my conviction is "stubborn"
My decisions are now "haste"
And I speak too much "wiThOuT rEsTraiNt"
What a waste
Like the bottom of the ocean hiding a precious pearl
What a waste it is to be a powerful woman
In a broken man's world

Write a piece about

Women

A woman is to divinity
What the sun is to the earth
More than a being
She is a portal for the spirit world
An incubator
God-level mortal
Birthing self onto self
The seed is also divine
But only in the way
the moon
is divine to the tides
For a son cannot give birth
So a woman is to divinity
What the sun is to the earth

Write a piece about

Dedication

I afford no room in my life for a man with no passion
I used to want to help
Help breathe life into the broken compass of the wandering
But a maternal tendency with this kind of goblin partner
borders an incestuous garden
where resentment grows
between the seeds of a future
neither will ever see
Unless he is dedicated to a goal he deems golden
He should have no eyes for me

Write a piece about

College

I lose myself in a book
the way candy melts in a mouth
And stare at sheets of processed wood for hours
and hours and hours
Seeking knowledge for the soul
to understand the world I'm in
Politics and holy books
And sheets that Carl Jung confided in
But this reality is ironic
Considering how much I hated school
How much I hated most teachers
And how much I still hate rules
Yet I can't help but wonder
if my love of books is just a ploy
subconsciously compensating for diploma papers
that I rejected to play with noise

Write a piece about

Lack of motivation

I'm sorry, but I no longer
have sympathy for this
Every shot that you don't take
is bound to be a miss
Every night in self-pity
is an opportunity lost
to build a kingdom from the ruins
and set fire to the frost
No one's coming in to help you
It's you or you or you
Can't change the cards that you've been dealt
playing them is all that you can do
Truth is that in this life
everyone is not meant to win
But winners failed a hundred times—
they just weren't afraid to try again

Write a piece about

Positions

The sun is only the sun to the daylight
But to the night sky,
the sun is nothing but a fable
A fairy tale it's never seen
A fairy tale that's never been
I remember that
every time I think of how you couldn't see me for everything I was
Our positions in the stars just weren't aligned
How could I fault the night sky
for thinking the morning sun was just a lie?

> **Write a piece about**
> **Starting a new career later in life**

Do not burden yourself with the judgments of others
Jump headfirst into chance
With the expectation of being embraced
Because just as we make humans flinch
and extend their arms out
when we jolt forward
the universe flinches too
So jump.

Write a piece about

Writing a song

Imagine Adam assuming
he was the last of God's creations
Imagine the horse assuming
he was "it" for far locations
There is a false sense of importance
that veils a virgin muse
when they assume that they're the masterpiece
when they're just the brush I use
I've written songs about my first love
And I will write songs about my last
I've written songs about my dancing future
And I'll write songs about my limping past
So to anyone grandiose
Thinking "she wrote that about me"
The last four lines are just for you
Hope you thoroughly enjoy the read
Your self-importance should've never weighed
on the songs I might've made you
Divinity in my world is only yours
as long as I decide to paint you

Write a piece about

Witchcraft

I can't help my relationship with spirit
And you can't help the fear it ignites
I can't help that my dreams are as clear as a movie
Or that my future reality is often just as precise
I can't help that my tongue is a wand
And that I do exactly what I said I would do
I can't help that the heavens all galvanize
To make sure all my visions come true
I can't help that somehow I hear what you think
And see motives from light years away
So the only advice I can give you
when dealing with me
Is to mean what you say

Write a piece about

Trying to be authentic in a foreign language

My tongue is tied by the limitations of my geography
Because if I could turn into water
and run like a river into every town of the world
I would
If strangers could drink me and I could soothe their hearts
like a godly elixir
I would
If I could bear my burdens and ungown my ugly
to the point of eliciting peace
because they could see their own demons in me
and would no longer feel alone
I would
But I can't
Luckily
Music is universal
So I do what I can
And sing my truth
Hoping that the Melody carries my spirit
And hoping that the greater good uses me
And selfishly
Maybe in doing as much good as I can
One day
My bruises will leave
And one day
My pain will ease
And one day
I'll find my peace

> **Write a piece about**
>
> **Jessie Reyez**

Time for goodbye
My body is beat
Eyelids finally droppin'
A bitch needa sleep
Night lol

ACKNOWLEDGMENTS

Thank you to God. Thank you to my mom and dad for allowing the creativity in me to survive.

Special thank you to my executive assistant Camila Bravo for bearing with me and my hundreds of emails and edits in this jungle of paper we carved into a book.

Thank you to my FMLY team: Byron Wilson, Jermi Thomas, Jessica Nyland, and Anil Rana; WME; Andrews McMeel; and Simon & Schuster. Thank you to Haley Heidemann and my incredible agent Zach Iser. My dog.

Special thank you to my editor, Danys Mares, for not losing your mind every time I said "final note," which was followed by more emails with more notes.

And lastly, and again, thank you to my motherfucking self.

ABOUT THE AUTHOR

Jessie Reyez burns bright.

Serving as a light in the dark for a legion of loyal fans, Jessie channels her lived experiences and remarkable empathy into cathartic artistry. Celebrated as a songwriter, recording artist, live performer, philanthropist, activist, and author, Jessie is cementing her status as a storyteller across mediums.

Jessie Reyez was born in Toronto, Canada, to Colombian immigrants and was raised between worlds. Linguistically and culturally fluid, Jessie has always had music as a universal grounding point. Taught guitar by her father at a young age, Jessie would explore various means of expression from instruments to voice to dance; poetry, however, was always her first love. Whether performing on festival stages, speaking in intimate interviews, or gracing live television, Jessie connects deeply with her words. A prolific writer, she captures the human experience in a way that is at once unique and relatable. Her sparks turn to wildfires that burn down decay and make space for beauty to bloom again. Outside of her own songs, she has lent her talents to others, penning records for the likes of Calvin Harris, Dua Lipa, Sam Smith, and Kehlani.

Today, Jessie has already enjoyed a storied career as a recording artist. After releasing critically acclaimed EPs (*Kiddo* and *Being Human in Public*) and albums (*Before Love Came to Kill Us* and *YESSIE*) that have accumulated over three billion streams, the Grammy-nominated, multiple Juno Award–winning, multiplatinum selling, Billboard Women in Music Impact Award recipient, MTV Video Music Award–nominated phenom is stepping back from the microphone and out of her comfort zone, starting again at the bottom of a new profession.

A hopeful romantic with a history of heartbreak, Jessie cuts deep to the bone with her writing and bares raw emotion. *Words of a Goat Princess* Vol I and II are not blueprints on how to get over a broken heart, but rather an extension of Jessie's ongoing dialogue with the self and her latest attempt to reconcile idealism and experience.

Jessie is a global citizen, and her words have resounded across every continent on the map. Jessie's days alternating between touring and escaping have allowed her to soak up the human condition in all of its joy, misery, excitement, and banality. Her prized possessions are her memories, and her most precious moments are with her family.

Jessie Reyez currently splits her time between Toronto, Canada, and Los Angeles, California.

ABOUT THE ILLUSTRATOR

Braktosaure (Eloïse Diot), a French Caribbean illustrator from Guadeloupe, thrives in capturing moods through her unique and evocative artwork.

With a style that blends darkness and naivety, she translates raw emotions through touching characters, inviting viewers to embark on a journey of self-reflection.

Her art features imperfect lines and a special affinity for black and white, adding to the emotional resonance.

You may recognize her work from her contributions to the artwork on Jessie Reyez's critically acclaimed project *Being Human in Public*.

Immersing oneself in Braktosaure's universe calls for a cathartic introspection within the beautifully melancholic world she creates.

INDEX

*The original fan-submitted prompt for each poem can be found at the page number in parenthesis.

Abandonment 47 (x)
A curse 160 (154)
A dead leaf on the ground 116 (114)
A face looking like a seat 7 (x)
A grassy field 146 (115)
Air 53 (58)
Alcohol 122 (114)
Alignment 141 (114)
An untouched river in the jungle 76 (59)
Are you afraid dumbasses are going to try to steal these to use as lyrics? 159 (155)
Attachment 16 (1)
Becoming the best version of yourself 18 (1)
Being famous 106 (59)
Being mentally damaged 121 (115)
Being understood 162 (155)
Big butts 55 (x)
Boys who think it's OK to come in and out of your life like it's no biggie 25 (1)
Breadcrumbs 42 (x)
Breaking generational trauma 143 (115)
Child eyes 64 (59)
College 176 (155)
Control 69 (58)
Cutting ties w/ that one person 36 (x)
Dedication 174 (155)
Devotion 2 (1)
Distance 161 (155)
Dreaming you're back in high school again 94 (58)
Earthquakes 39 (1)
Eating a sour fruit 135 (114)
Fate 74 (58)
Father-daughter love 70 (154)
Feeling like you always need more from life 149 (114)
Feeling stuck but everyone thinks you are moving forward 22 (1)

Finally being able to feel happiness after years 110 (58)
Financial struggles 112 (viii)
Finding happiness 77 (58)
Finding the one 50 (viii)
Fitting better than blue jeans 24 (x)
Forgiving yourself 31 (x)
Free Palestine 78 (58)
Gaslighting 66 (59)
Geminis 84 (58)
Graffiti on the side of the highway: "The more I think about it, the bigger it gets" 118 (114)
Grief 49 (viii)
Grief II 57 (viii)
Grounding 147 (115)
Growling up 150 (114)
Guilt 83 (58)
Hatred 127 (115)
Healing generational wounds 144 (115)
Hope 128 (115)
How I can't fall in love with nobody 20 (x)
How the waves kiss your feet? 10 (x)
Infatuation 23 (115)
Jessie Reyez 185 (155)
Lack of motivation 177 (154)
Laziness 100 (58)
Limerence 29 (x)
Loneliness 88 (59)
Long-distance relationships 30 (viii)
Looking into someone's eyes and feeling peace and happiness 86 (viii)
Los Angeles, California 164 (154)
Losing a child 90 (59)
Love 44 (114)
Loving someone that loves someone else 26 (1)
Marriage 15 (x)
Mental gymnastics 134 (115)
Mind-blowing things 43 (154)

Missing someone too much 113 (x)
Monstrosity 130 (114)
Mothers 93 (58)
Mourning 61 (59)
Moving through fear 105 (154)
No contact 46 (viii)
Nostalgia 89 (58)
Not being able to cry or access your sadness 133 (114)
Not having community 63 (58)
Obsession 41 (1)
People watching on the subway platform 104 (59)
Perseverance 163 (155)
Poema sobre no haberte enamorado nunca, no haber tenido pareja 19 (1)
Poems or something? Let me not be bossy 172 (154)
Politics. Sucks but why refugees are treated differently depending on the narrative 96 (59)
Positions 178 (155)
Pride 27 (x)
Purgatory 95 (58)
Queerness 124 (114)
Realizing you wasted your youth 107 (viii)
Reconnecting w/ an old love 13 (154)
Redemption 32 (x)
Rewriting the stars 6 (x)
Right person wrong time 14 (154)
Rivers 109 (58)
Seeing someone beyond their physical appearance 11 (1)
Self-doubt 148 (115)
Serenity 56 (x)
Sleep 97 (59)
Small victories 99 (59)
Space 102 (58)
Spirit animals 167 (155)
Standing on the beach at sunset 40 (1)
Standing your ground 152 (115)
Starting a new career later in life 179 (155)

Staying quiet when someone insults you 85 (viii)
Stubbing your toe on the table when you were having a good day 111 (155)
Success 168 (155)
That feeling you get right before you jump off of a cliff/boat into water 136 (114)
The "avoidant" attachment 137 (114)
The brain inside your stomach. Gut feels. 140 (115)
The deep connection we have with some people not knowing why 51 (1)
The feeling when you write 170 (154)
The guy who introduced me to your music and then ghosted me two months later 52 (viii)
The meaning of life 60 (59)
The moon 156 (154)
The news 103 (59)
The psychology of your own brain 138 (114)
The unknown infinite vastness of the universe 73 (155)
The way imagination is considered something for kids only 169 (154)
Tranquility 72 (59)
Trying to be authentic in a foreign language 183 (154)
Unrequired love 8 (x)
Using your weakness against you 4 (1)
Wanting to fall apart in someone's arms but can't 34 (x)
Whether or not you're OK 120 (115)
Witchcraft 182 (154)
Witchy women being burned at the stake 142 (114)
Women 173 (155)
Worth 153 (114)
Writer's block 158 (154)
Writing a song 180 (154)
Your future husband 48 (viii)
Your life 80 (viii)
Your mental state atm 119 (115)

The People's Purge copyright © 2025 by Jessie Reyez. All rights reserved. Printed in China. No part of this book may be used or reproduced in any manner whatsoever without written permission, except in the case of reprints in the context of reviews.

The authorised representative in the EEA is Simon and Schuster Netherlands BV, Herculesplein 96 3584 AA Utrecht, Netherlands. (info@simonandschuster.nl)

Andrews McMeel Publishing
a division of Andrews McMeel Universal
1130 Walnut Street, Kansas City, Missouri 64106

www.andrewsmcmeel.com

25 26 27 28 29 SDB 10 9 8 7 6 5 4 3 2 1

ISBN: 979-8-8816-0465-3

Library of Congress Control Number: 2025937237

Editor: Danys Mares
Art Director: Holly Swayne
Production Editor: Dave Shaw
Production Manager: Julie Skalla

ATTENTION: SCHOOLS AND BUSINESSES
Andrews McMeel books are available at quantity discounts with bulk purchase for educational, business, or sales promotional use. For information, please email the Andrews McMeel Publishing Special Sales Department: sales@andrewsmcmeel.com.

 Enjoy *The People's Purge* as an audiobook narrated by the author, wherever audiobooks are sold.